MADAME X

ALSO BY WILLIAM LOGAN

POETRY

Sad-Faced Men (1982)
Difficulty (1985)
Sullen Weedy Lakes (1988)
Vain Empires (1998)
Night Battle (1999)
Macbeth in Venice (2003)
The Whispering Gallery (2005)
Strange Flesh (2008)
Deception Island: Selected Early Poems, 1974–1999 (2011)

CRITICISM

All the Rage (1998)
Reputations of the Tongue (1999)
Desperate Measures (2002)
The Undiscovered Country (2005)
Our Savage Art (2009)

PENGUIN POETS

WILLIAM LOGAN

MADAME X

PENGUIN BOOKS

Published by the Penguin Group

Penguin Group (USA) Inc., 375 Hudson Street, New York, New York 10014, U.S.A.
Penguin Group (Canada), 90 Eglinton Avenue East, Suite 700,
Toronto, Ontario, Canada M4P 2Y3 (a division of Pearson Penguin Canada Inc.)
Penguin Books Ltd, 80 Strand, London WC2R 0RL, England
Penguin Ireland, 25 St Stephen's Green, Dublin 2, Ireland (a division of Penguin Books Ltd)
Penguin Group (Australia), 250 Camberwell Road, Camberwell, Victoria 3124, Australia
(a division of Pearson Australia Group Pty Ltd)
Penguin Books India Pvt Ltd, 11 Community Centre, Panchsheel Park, New Delhi - 110 017, India
Penguin Group (NZ), 67 Apollo Drive, Rosedale, Auckland 0632, New Zealand
(a division of Pearson New Zealand Ltd)
Penguin Books (South Africa) (Pty) Ltd, 24 Sturdee Avenue,
Rosebank, Johannesburg 2196, South Africa

Penguin Books Ltd, Registered Offices:
80 Strand, London WC2R 0RL, England

First published in Penguin Books 2012

1   3   5   7   9   10   8   6   4   2

Copyright © William Logan, 2012
All rights reserved

Pages xi and xii constitute an extension of this copyright page.

LIBRARY OF CONGRESS CATALOGING IN PUBLICATION DATA
Logan, William, 1950 Nov. 16–
Madame X / William Logan.
p. cm.—(Penguin Poets)
Poems.
ISBN 978-0-14-312238-8
I. Title.
PS3562.O449M33 2012
811'.54—dc2   2012023584

Printed in the United States of America
Set in Adobe Garamond
Designed by Catherine Leonardo

For Sharon Dunn and Collette Adams

CONTENTS

I

II / THE GILDED AGE

III

IV / THE BRONZE AGE

V

Acknowledgments

Birmingham Poetry Review: August Rhapsody; Dies Irae; The South in the South; *Carolina Quarterly:* On the Suburbs; *Cincinnati Review:* D-Day; *Columbia:* Atlantic Ocean. Winter. 1954.; Siringo in the Appalachians; *Gettysburg Review:* Spring Run Aground; *Harvard Review:* The Field; *Hopkins Review:* Book Thirteen; *Kenyon Review:* The Imitation of Things Familiar; Winter Without Memory; *Little Star:* The Sunny South; *Modern Review:* RSVP; *New Criterion:* A Death at Badenweiler; The Old Story; Summer in the High Purpose of Clouds; *New England Review:* Leap Year; The War, the War; *New Republic:* In the Confining Hour; *New York Sun:* Sodom; *New Yorker:* Any Old Kind of Aunt; For an Old Girlfriend, Long Dead; Geckos in Obscure Light; *Notre Dame Review:* And Now for Something Completely Different; The Crane Among Its Minions; The Fens as an Action of Grace; *Poetry:* The Eels of the Lagoon; On the Wood Storks;

The Other Place; Trespassing; *Poetry Northwest:* Blues; Spring on the Bill of Lading; *Salmagundi:* Along the Autumn River; Henry James Visiting Ashburton Place, 1904; London. High Summer.; To the Ghost of an Old Girlfriend; *Sewanee Review:* General Custer on New York Island; Lady Hester Stanhope; Mrs. Custer in Washington City; Spring On Guard; *Smartish Pace:* After Sappho 58; *Southwest Review:* Madame X; *32 Poems:* After Sappho 31; *TLS:* By the Closed Museum; The Hedgehog in His Element; On the Hedgehog; Spring in Odd Weather; Winter in the Old School; *Warwick Review:* Dolores; *Yale Review:* The Back of a Girl in Florence; Spring in the Preliminaries; Winter of Falling Temperature.

"Four Fragments of the *Odyssey*" first appeared in *Homer in English,* ed. George Steiner (Penguin, 1996).

MADAME X

Socially, Ahab was inaccessible. Though nominally included in the census of Christendom, he was still an alien to it. He lived in the world, as the last of the Grisly Bears lived in settled Missouri. And as when Spring and Summer had departed, that wild Logan of the woods, burying himself in the hollow of a tree, lived out the winter there, sucking his own paws; so, in his inclement, howling old age, Ahab's soul, shut up in the caved trunk of his body, there fed upon the sullen paws of its gloom!

—*MOBY-DICK*

Keep your mind off the poetry and on the pajamas and everything will be all right.

—GREGORY PECK IN *ROMAN HOLIDAY*

I

THE HEDGEHOG IN HIS ELEMENT

Miserable, bullying, armed to the teeth,
like a Sherman tank forced out of the brush
or St. Sebastian bristling with arrows.

SPRING ON THE BILL OF LADING

There grew a confusion in the chrome-yellow crease
through storm clouds, on the tarnished silver fields.

Arched trees lay in a scribble of nightfall.
May had brought Impressionism's paid-for agenda,

peace filling the muddy ditches, at a price.
Bomb fragments steeped with turnips in the furrows;

the new potatoes nestled a rusty grenade.
The tidal sky shut down like a gray wave.

Some dawns, a single-minded crow kept watch
on brazen clouds lit like chinked edges of shields.

The sudden mirror of a stream repaired
the cold narcissus beds. Our frail sun faltered,

a halogen bulb beneath the proud scar-tissue,
one amputated flare, then the absent dark.

THE FENS AS AN ACTION OF GRACE

The calm settles lightly on grasses, limestone knobs,
the fall of a rail line proved like a Roman road,
as if it knew where its best interests lay, but were
        in no particular hurry to get there.

Yanked on a cord, the startled pheasant
knows nature by nature is obscene.
What of the irreverent farmhouse,
        the callous vans, the calm and curious clouds?

These too have their place, if only
to be scraped from the picture at last.
There is a stoniness beyond even these,
        requiring the flicker and scent of ceremony,

or catalogues cool in their atonements,
or merely a bush speaking in tongues.

Madame X

John Singer Sargent, *Madame X*

Visitors scarcely glance at her now as they pass by.
I imagine a half-audible sigh

escaping her pursed and self-confiding lips
like the thrum of certain stately ships

that, having weighed anchor, never come to port.
Her feelings, no doubt, were of the finer sort.

In modesty's immodesty, she averts her gaze
through the crackled oil's concealing haze,

a woman who touched up her ears with lavender powder,
her skin the shade of Delmonico's clam chowder,

the waist pinched narrow as a wasp's,
not cinched tight until you could hear her gasp,

her dress exposing, in cold décolletage,
the Alpine-slope breasts, which were briefly the rage.

Hers was sometimes called a professional beauty,
which implies a certain impersonal duty

to a beauty evanescent as morning vapor.
The painter thought her face like blotting paper.

You can see, alas, how it would end.
Those who rise so high rarely have grace to descend.

A century on, my students' low-cut jeans
have the effect of a match on gasoline,

flaunting like a cold slice of mutton
a naked four inches below the belly button,

a strip of flesh that asks the old question.
(Is nothing more sexual than a taste for suggestion?)

Poor Madame X, in her day, was far bolder—
originally the right strap had slipped off her shoulder.

By the Closed Museum

The lions faced away from the noble Greek
criminal pillars, guarding what stood behind them.

A cream stain seeped over the museum,
a shade Cotman would have envied.

His greens gnawed the excavated walks.
We wavered beneath the bold, judicial chestnut

while the world burned in silver, more or less,
and looked backward at that other world.

There remained the fast-forward rush to escape
the salvations by which we were burdened.

SPRING IN ODD WEATHER

Not the dampness of opportunity, perhaps;
nor an irritating jumble of stimuli, choreographed

by some renegade Balanchine; nor
the particular razory liaison of May rain,

enough to muzzle the tits in the greening hedge;
nor the lofty bloat of ruined cloud

stalking the placid rape-fields, which still
awaited an eighteenth-century painter

who had failed to show; no, these, not even these
could account for the whicker of spring chill,

Commerce that muzzled her admirers in Art,
though above the fens, on the raw silhouette

of a hill—tentative, new-risen with weeds
like Iron Age spears—you stood your watch,

staring out in something like astonishment,
a porcelain doll blank in its own gaze.

IN THE CONFINING HOUR

In the confining hour, in the revealing place,
comes the heart's glottal stop, comes the lie's restless face.

On the resistant deck, on the consoling floor,
rolls the meadowed plain, rolls the forgotten war.

There stand the bills unpaid, there the fates unmet—
send for the butcher's price, send for love's regret.

Blow wind from north, blow rain from south,
pay for the marble kiss, pay the proxy mouth.

For the confirming rod, for the concealing dress,
bring on the shadow's bloom, bring the false caress.

SPRING ON GUARD

Spring is our blackness, our *rouge et noir*.
The flowers droop like revolution's flags,
ragged, disturbed by dry wind, whipped to passion
like the flare of lost aristocratic love.
We take our beauty sleep in fits and starts,
crawling, as in a dream, backward toward fish life.
After so many years, what words are left?
The sparrows bolt, a mob of Persian soldiers,
and through the scattered night a black slug crawls,
horned like a samurai helmet's thin brass moon.
We stare like sphinxes at the vanishing point.
Sometimes the dawn comes up, and sometimes not,
old devil-worshipped ball of gas, at last
clearing the eastern rooftops in a glaze.

And Now for Something Completely Different

In the room, the television blazes
as a fire used to, homely and open to reason.
I peer into it, as a god would—

no wonder I feel there should be a soul.
I saw her once,
when I was nineteen and relentless.

She was just a girl in a yellow dress,
to whom life had yet to happen.
Now it had happened.

I too would have refused to speak
to the living. She wanted to be more than she was.
I wanted to be Achilles.

For an Old Girlfriend, Long Dead

Lying on that blanket, nights on the seventh green—
in the dry air the scent of gasoline,

nothing above us but the ragged moon,
nothing between but a whispered *soon* . . .

Well, such was romance in the seventies.
Watergate and Cambodia, the public lies,

made our love seem, somehow, more true.
Of the few things I wanted then, I needed you.

I remember our last arguments, the angry calls,
then the long silence, those northern falls

we drifted toward our newly manufactured lives.
Does anything else of us survive?

That day in Paris, perhaps, when you swore
our crummy hotel was all you were looking for—

each cobbled street, each dry baguette,
even the worthless *sous* nothing you'd forget.

Outside, a block away, the endless Seine
flowed roughly, then brightly, then . . .

Then nothing. Nothing later went quite that far.
I remember that spring. Those breasts. That car.

GECKOS IN OBSCURE LIGHT

Tentative, greedy, by night they came,
drawn to the insects drawn to the light.

Their shadow organs pulsed
beneath bellies distended as Falstaff's,

backs a tarnished armor studded
by the rosettes of some obscure disease.

What of their victims, the cannon fodder,
Welsh soldiery thrown each night

against the muzzle flare? Ragged, high-strung moths,
green lacewings streamlined like F-16s—

the geckos, those great officers and kings,
took them into their mouths, more or less

at leisure, with a gratifying snap.
Silently, of course, through the pane of glass,

where death comes on a smaller scale.

Sodom

Storm light. The parched musical howl.
The west returned a sickly glow,
like a liqueur trickled down the gray pages.

That neural aftermath weather,
the marshes whipped themselves to an acid froth,
as if they knew the sin of charity,

as if God had disapproved of the blueprints
and thrown down a few hurricanes
to batter the docks, make matchsticks

of the heavily mortgaged condominiums.
Placid palms threw themselves this way and that,
as if trying out for a chorus line.

THE WAR, THE WAR

The heavy-lidded wood storks
wade the retention pond like a chain gang,
single file, the blanket of algae

clearing before them and closing in behind.
Pale blossoms, chipped like teacups,
grace the magnolia slumping

over brackish waters. The bougainvillea,
the reek of jasmine, the blurred petals
in jardinieres—wasn't the garden

a corner of Paradise ready to be recycled?
Is that an idea dangling
from the telephone wires?

No, just more kudzu vines,
spiraling nowhere, scribbled by someone
who could not color between the lines.

In the flea market, you spied,
mounted high on a pegboard, like a trophy
in Odysseus's hall, an AK-47 made of wood.

LEAP YEAR

The windows were stained yellow with pollen,
the dogwood fringed with punkish pink froth.

Azaleas offered their wounded,
crumpled blossoms, scribbled and half erased.

Each view had been submitted to the *salon des refusés*.
The sandhill cranes were planning to leave town,

their choked, metallic cries on the air,
like car alarms banging through a distant neighborhood.

Deep in the prairie, alligators got down to business—
mating, or seeking a mate, or getting a quickie divorce,

reptiles with the morals of Wall Street
and an address in the Cretaceous.

Like a zombie, I walked behind four girls,
each with a tattoo in the small of her back.

An advertisement for sex, doggy style,
or just something for the man of her dreams?

Love, the word and the thing, the only *ding an sich*.

SPRING IN THE PRELIMINARIES

That awkward hour, the beautiful was loose.
God strutted beneath the live oaks, eyes pinched shut,
the season on his hands like day-old bread.
What was sin then but a shadow on the grass?

Like dog-eared pages, new leaves marked their place,
blurred rage of spring's small paralyzed arousals,
the batteries charged and glowing for the task.
Beneath the method of the mockingbirds,

each azalea offered a democracy,
the crowds of flowers smoldering after rain,
the swamp frogs touting their muddy real estate.

I watched the girls' small breasts, like raw pink buds,
new pollen dusting the myopic lens.
The sun went dark, guttered, lit up again.

The Eels of the Lagoon

I am not sure, even now, what troubled me
about the eels. Fifty years ago, I was forced
to leave a whaling village whose saltbox houses
shored against the salt-hay fields
in bleached, frigid, miserable emptiness . . .
the wavering line of dunes, the swollen river, the blank ocean.
In the dim corridor of the shingled wharf,
the light caught, refracted by dusty panes,
watery troughs lifting the catch of thin-shelled steamers;
gladiatorial lobsters, their lumpish claws pinned
by wooden wedges; mussels the forbidden indigo
of twilight. From the sweatered neck of a clam
jetted forth a stinging, whispery stream
of salt water, baptizing me in the eye.

I was still a stranger to Venice then.
The first time I viewed that floating world,
the Grand Canal was plumed in frozen mist,
a curtain of fog aslant the corrugated waters,
as if closing on an old, rarely applauded play.
Across from the flaking bandbox of Ca' d'Oro,
the fishmongers had just opened their stalls.
The market's columns, squatter than the common
Palladian orders, were carved no later
than my father's father's time. The past
makes its small homages, as it must,
even in such a *capriccio* of the Jazz Age,
the stone capitals elaborately chiseled
into the hulls of wherries, grimacing visages
of octopus and squid, agreeable monsters of the lagoon,
guardians to protect the salty turns of commerce.

I smelled then the old desire. The salty stink,
the nearness of the ocean's flesh, filled me
with an abiding—I am ashamed to admit—
nostalgia for *it*, the unnamed and unreachable *it*,
the *it* of those early voiceless scenes. What ransoms
must they require, childhood and its losses?
Having sought them in the fish markets
of Istanbul and Paris, I waited for that slightly foul,
antiquated odor to return me again
to those seeping reliquaries, so that once more
I might enter Paradise.
                              That morning, all came to view:
the placid tuna hacked into agate slabs;
the warty, demonic bottom fish slumped in mortal piles;
an upended crab flailing a stiffened claw.
Off to one side, in a stainless-steel tray, for sale
like the rest, like glistening bejeweled intestines,
lay man's first great tempter and antagonist,
the serpent. Of course, these weren't serpents
dead before me, merely common eels,
mud-feeders, greasy, tough as rawhide,
a *nature morte* fetched by some jobbing
Sienese painter. Just beyond the tray
lay the glinting knife, the pile of skinned
and eviscerated carcasses, even the rough skins,
like Michelangelo's oily, sloughed-off rag
held up in the Sistine Chapel. Silence
rose from the blood-smeared block,
where all had grown still. Then one of the bodies
slid against its neighbor, and all gruesomely turned
together, like the terrible gears of a clock.

Recalling this now, I am not sure I have caught
their sad composure, their curious complaisance,
as if they had suffered all this before,
though even worse than the dying was the watching.

II

THE GILDED AGE

MRS. CUSTER IN WASHINGTON CITY

September, 1864

My Darling—

    This is the saddest city,
the maimed and bandaged soldiers mobbing the streets.
    Slow-moving government hearses pass,
        the black coffins
    wrapped in the flag these boys died for.
Painted establishments embalming the dead

    are planted on each corner.
Old Mr. K. stopped here last night, most cordial.
    Too much so, for I had to avoid
        his bold attempt
    to kiss me, by gripping a chair.
This city is a Sodom, crowded with sin,

    by day as well as by night.
Small bands of ragged Secessionists still weave
    through our half-rebel city, yet there
        is a fine show
of patriotism. Our flag
stretches across the street, and darkeys parade,

    dressed in bold and gaudy hues,
unused to liberty, in proud procession,
    faces tinted pale to sooty black.
        Their babies have
    beady eyes and black woolly heads.
(They are all so *good*—I never heard one cry.)

All the avenues have filled
with gilded sin, some girls wearing their dresses
    suspiciously long. Even though I
            despise a veil,
        I might as well live in Turkey,
for I dare not go out alone without one.

    My lodging house sits between
a Lincoln flag (I am quite a Lincoln girl)
        and a banner with McClellan's name.
                As soldiers pass,
            they raise a cheer for McClellan
and groan for poor Lincoln, or just the reverse!

    The President, that great soul,
is the gloomiest, most painfully careworn
        man I ever saw. If McClellan
                were elected,
            that would mean peace—dishonest peace,
perhaps. Autie, I want peace on any terms.

        It may be unwomanly—
much as I love my country, I love you more.
        Why must your Brigade do everything?
                My canary
            notepaper says I'm cavalry.
I have trimmed a hat with cavalry yellow.

                        Your dear little Army crow,

                        Libbie

GENERAL CUSTER ON NEW YORK ISLAND

April, 1866

Dear Old Sweetness—

        I am *so* lonesome.
You know how fond your boy is of the theater
        and of course you imagine me
a nightly attendant, but a certain Somebody
        is not here to go with me.

        I am in demand
with artists of all sorts—cast of head for bust,
        Miss Vinnie Ream for medallion,
&c. &c. Three of us started
        with Colonel Howe down Broadway

        in a blue carriage,
thence into Wall Street, where I was introduced
        to prominent capitalists.
One proposed three cheers for Major-General Custer.
        Not three, but six, were given,

        and *with a tiger.*
Yet I should like to look for some new pursuit.
        Shall I obtain the position
of Foreign Minister, with a salary in gold
        of seven to ten thousand?

        About Washington—
when Andy is as upright as a tombstone,
        then day by day my confidence
in the Constitution increases. There is no news
        of a sober speech lately,

but I am nightly
expecting some grand and peculiar outburst
        of what he styles his eloquence.
Unlike some public characters, he does not swallow
        the gristle of his own words.

                Our great bal masqué
will be reported in the *Harper's Weekly*.
        Your boy was the only Devil
in the staid halls of the Academy of Music,
        my costume of red silk tights

                and no drawers beneath,
a red cap with two upright feathers for horns,
        and a small mask of blackest silk.
The matinée with Miss Kellogg in *Faust* was *superb*.
        After, we old officers

                went on a brief scout,
visiting several shooting galleries
        and pretty-girl-waitress saloons.
We also had considerable sport with females—
        "nymphes du pavé" they are called.

                An art gallery
showed *Oriental Princess after the Bath*,
        a painting quite good in its way
but calculated to make the poorest schoolgirl blush.
        The wife of Senator C.

said that from hearsay
she inferred you a beauty—I said you were
        by *actual* observation.
Birds of all colors are worn in the center of fans.
        There's a new style of hair-nets.

                    Your own dear boy,

                    Autie

SIRINGO IN THE APPALACHIANS

I went into the large front room to drink "moonshine" . . . and to
watch the young folks play a new kind of a kissing game. . . . The one
snapped at would jump up and catch the snapper and by force kiss
him or her. I noticed that the kissing was always on the cheek.
—CHARLES SIRINGO, *A COWBOY DETECTIVE*

"Snap them there fingers," I warned her,
"and you'll wind up
with a western scientific kiss,
planted where she might do a real lick of good."
Later, that physic hanging off the lips
of this wretch of a sinner,

some sort of lice-bearded feudist
(his father plugged
by the Potter gang) stepped to the porch
like iced Death, grinning down on me face to face:
"Pilgrim, how would you like your goddamned *brains*
scattered on the floor?" said he.

I touched the old Hardin scabbard.
"Well, now," said I,
"I guess that there won't feel nice at all,
and these little gals would have to scrub them off."
The wretch opened up in some vulgar song,
its burden some thorny oath.

A real Texan—father, brother,
                even sweetheart—
would have filled his hide so full of balls,
you'd have needed that great-assed beast of Bunyan's
        to fetch his flyblown corpse to the boneyard.
                I needed to hightail it

                away from those clove-hitched cousins'
                        cross-eyed babies,
        and from the rotten noise of banjos.
Every household had half a dozen of such
        "instruments," each with its idiot boy
                picking out the same damned tune.

III

D-Day

The helmets bobbled in the surf,
upended thimbles of suds and blood.

THE SUNNY SOUTH

O fowls of air, O beasts of sea, O flies,
Paradise came at a discount, shrink-wrapped.

The lead sky rose like a clean slate,
the tin roofs nippled with aluminum.

The gray-green foliage slumped, shadowy,
beneath the wash of a vanished hurricane,

its course a straggling vine upon the Atlantic.
We were blasphemous and fowl-tongued,

gooselike souls whose honesties had burrowed
into the heartwood. The body had had its day.

I returned, an accidental warrior,
or accident-prone, the more welcome for that.

THE SOUTH IN THE SOUTH

Tree frogs mount a chorus in the water oaks,
a minor barrage of horns à la Herr Handel.

Even the snakes have turned petit bourgeois.
Yellow in throat

and irritable in disposition, the pig frogs
crank away in the artificial stone-pond.

Broken upon the wheel when young—
that would be metaphysical.

It is the South, after all.
We love martyrs here,

says the defrocked preacher.

ANY OLD KIND OF AUNT

She was the most ordinary aunt,
her saltbox choked with a hundred plants,

as if an overgrown garden had forced its way inside.
Dressed in white, like some antique bride,

she spent hours watering that jungle paradise.
It was, perhaps, her most obvious vice.

What was the ruined velvety gloom
that rose in the corner of the sewing room—

the black-frocked ghost of Henry James's vastation,
or just the shadow of an old indigestion?

Her floors were painted a cruel shade of lead.
Her kitchen belonged in the Smithsonian, my father said.

In one corner hunkered Ben Franklin's original stove.
A flock of iron pans hung precariously above,

like the wild headdress of an African queen.
Afternoons in her rocker, cleaning her runner beans,

my aunt glared at the oven's stiff black door
that stared with its isinglass eye, a grand inquisitor.

The only history in her family, like a dirty sock,
was a threadbare connection to Plymouth Rock

and, in her parlor, Daniel Webster's couch
squatting beneath bay windows in a fetal crouch.

Those stifling Fourths, past her rusting cars,
our sparklers cast down incandescent stars.

THE FIELD

Without regard for the mason's art,
only the dry mercies of gravity,

the ungainly loaf-shaped rocks
balanced on the border of the field.

Slash pines had long invaded
that sloping acre of weeds

my father had cleared with a sickle.
(*Why*, my mother said, *it could have become*

a gas station . . . or, or, or anything.)
O perditions of the ordinary!

In that village, the names on the voters' rolls
steamed from one wintry century to another.

Once, behind the skunk cabbage
and the withering stream, I climbed

the jagged glacial rocks with the neighbor boy
and stood atop them, young conquistador!

At the imagined sound of a rattlesnake,
I fled back to that mown field

browning in summer heat,
and sanctuary, and emptiness.

Spring Run Aground

Becalmed in the loose days, calmer in storm,
we let the summer's thread slip our raw fingers,
nothing to praise, nothing to shoulder now.
You turned to nature when the fever subsided,
a single peony, like a spent planet,
waiting to bloom and rotting on the stem.
The garden everywhere repented confusion,
roses outscaling the rotten trellises,
the lawn a feathery infection of moss,
strawberries lost beneath the tenant weeds.
The house backs stood abandoned in storm light,
coal-black clouds massing off the D-Day coast,
lightning bolts lancing down in ghosts of rain,
invading England, Napoleon's lost dream.

SUMMER IN THE HIGH PURPOSE OF CLOUDS

From the porthole, a few fan-handed rays
staggered across night's mezzotint.
In medias res—a whole life passed through its middles.
Below lay unnatural clumps and hillocks,

deceptive as bas-relief, a view the Renaissance
could have prevented. On the horizon, dawn blossomed,
one stroke slashing above another, scarlet bands
laddering to emptiness. The clouds parted,

and below lay the firefly lights of a city
otherwise black, like a rift valley
where some civilization slept undisturbed.
A minute later, the scene had discomposed itself.

LONDON. HIGH SUMMER.

Trafalgar Square was gray with pigeons,
Lord Nelson still erect above the fray,
rustier now, lost
in his cloudy thought, while tourists

dragged themselves below,
never meeting eye to eye.
All Europe a heat wave, on the Underground
young girls, with their bare torsos

and effective breasts, showed off all they knew,
which was just enough, or not enough.
They cut the lust with a knife.
We were drowning, drowning in fair weather.

I'd spent weeks watching the fields
yellow with jaundice, the pheasants
tiptoe out uncertainly and bargain for grain.
That unreliable summer,

the tropics sent the Old World telegrams.
The abandoned trade routes were geometric,
rum in this direction, slaves in that,
all for one and one for commerce!

The great ships of the line had passed.
Out in Greenwich, huge, tilted, overpainted anchors
littered the lawns, as if the country had lain
too long underwater and could not float.

LADY HESTER STANHOPE

The Jamesian young man had come
to beard the English lioness in her den,
a mansion carved into a dry mountain in Lebanon—

Lady Hester, rising sixty, besieged by feral cats,
she who thought Byron a swollen adolescent.
("That dangerous thing," he had joked, "a female wit.")

Shipwrecked off Rhodes, she wrapped herself
like a Turk and never looked back.
Entered Palmyra, ruined Palmyra,

petals strewn across her path, heading a troop
of moth-eaten Bedouin, swarthy camels,
a bickering English doctor. Suffered:

gossip, bubonic plague, the itch of madness.
After a slight, demanded the heads
of the mountain peasants, then had their wives

dragged to the slave markets of Tripoli.
It was a world where a woman could still cut a dash,
but no longer in London. Said: *Here, if I sit*

under a tree and talk to a camel driver,
at least I hear good sense. She outlived one land
and did not survive long enough for the next.

Henry James Visiting Ashburton Place, 1904

The dome of the statehouse, gilded, sublime,
squatted upon the rooftops. Like a mothballed coat,
the street had withstood the appetites of time.

How the felt distance of the Civil War objected
to all that had intervened, been lost,
all that had died, never to be resurrected.

Weeks later, feeling again that obscure desire
to see where his career had begun its rise, its cost,
where the blank pages, etc., he found a wrecker's fire

and piles of rubble. He had known, the Master,
how fast history could be made. *I had doubtless,* he wrote,
never so felt that it could be unmade still faster.

Dolores

One vernal spring morning Prince Hitendra (of Cooch Behar) asked
me to marry him, but I was so startled . . . I forgot I was already mar-
ried, and told him bluntly I could never marry a black man.

Thus my almost relative, she of the vacant glance
and gypsy earrings, Epstein's favorite model
during the Vorticist phase, her plaster bust

consoling a face thumbed, heavy-lidded
or merely fashionably bored, and this no doubt
what recommended her, not just to Prince Hitendra

but to my great-great-uncle, veteran
of half a dozen two-reelers purporting to be westerns,
though filmed in the Adirondacks, the roles

allowing him to claim he had been raised
in a tepee and christened Young Buffalo,
which proved of some service in London

after the Great War, where he played cowboys,
later chewing scenery in the hustings,
on tour with companies year by year shabbier,

until at last he was hard up in Reading,
prone to what westerners called the "snakes,"
and accused of the murder

of one Alfred Oliver, tobacconist,
the case turning on a pair of bloodstained trousers
suspiciously laundered, the papers playing up

this melodrama, AMERICAN ACTOR
QUESTIONED IN MURDER, though in the end
he was never indicted, leading to triumphant scenes

upon a hotel balcony, then the decline
into a pea-soup fog of drink, libel suits,
some months running a London newsstand,

with nothing to delay the biographer's attention
but, a year after the murder, the brief notice
in *Time* announcing the engagement

of Young Buffalo and Dolores,
once the "most beautiful woman in London,"
not the result of some agent trying to wed

two small notorieties into a column of print,
but—and this at least kinder—the aftermath
of smoldering looks in a play called *The Monster*,

months as man and wife in a rooming house
in Dover (Dolores *already* married,
the bill unpaid), two damages finding something

not too distant from love,
she soon dead of cancer, but reduced before then
to appearing in a barrel at a fun fair

(SEE EPSTEIN'S FAMOUS MODEL!),
and now remembered only for a few busts
in regional museums, Young Buffalo

still prime suspect in a murder
unsolved, of mild fascination to crime buffs,
the outtakes affording him some measure

of posthumous fame, which, like a bad notice,
might have given a resting actor
some rueful pleasure, whether guilty or not.

Trespassing

That summer we were strangers in the house
of strangers, their garden pristine, merciless,

as if no one ever strolled its serpentine walks.
A lone magpie quarreled on a branch.

Secrets mossed the paving stones.
The larch sprouted glossy fingers of leaf,

pruned by some disembodied gardener.
We felt like antique servants, servants

who had become masters. The lives
of these strangers were no worse than ours—

perhaps they were even a little better,
lives where just enough happiness had been earned

and just enough sadness spent,
where hardly anyone was ever murdered

and the mail mostly came on time.

THE BACK OF A GIRL IN FLORENCE

> Nothing, like something, happens anywhere.
> —PHILIP LARKIN

Amsterdam, London, Paris, Basel, Rome,
I rode the trains with hippies, far from home

on their private Grand Tours, which as a rule
ended in Kabul, Kathmandu, or graduate school.

I passed the dusty porticos long closed,
a cobbled alley hung with women's clothes,

Venus de Milo, Nike of Samothrace,
those haunted galleries, each with its haunted face.

On a *rapido* through the *campagna*, stalled for hours
beside a field of homely saffron flowers,

I came to no great decision about my life,
had no epileptic idea, did not meet my future wife,

and later suffered no epiphanies beside the Parthenon,
no geologic insight reading Chesterton.

One evening in Florence, though, I walked
behind three blonde Americans, who talked

of the inconsequent nothings of their summer,
where everything was *Cool!* or *Far out!* or *Such a bummer!*

The tall pony-legged one, tanned and lithe,
marched with the instinct of a harvest scythe,

her long back naked beneath the evening's haze,
arched shoulder blades chiseled by Praxiteles.

What sculpture is more beautiful than a living breast,
an inturned belly, or hazel eyes that suggest

hopes new rendered, then forever lost?
We were young, of course, and that was the cost.

Had I approached, what would she have had to say,
that girl whose loveliness would soon decay?

I kept silent rather than take the risk.
O my Manet! My walking odalisque!

August Rhapsody

Last night the liver-colored sky

vaguely warned us, like a painted-over stop sign,
that our lives were half over, more likely two-thirds.
Life, that inattentive waiter,

was too eager to hand over the bill.
Yet why be gloomy when the roses have revived,
the St. John's wort resurrected itself

at the bottom of the garden?
The terra-cotta bust of a young Augustus
moons over the iris spears, a god

with an army to play with. Tra la.

IV

THE BRONZE AGE

BOOK THIRTEEN

A drink! A toast! To those who must die.
—CHRISTOPHER LOGUE

The buddleia struck its colors, the dawn
proving somewhat a disappointment, as so often.
Blood stained the sand beside cracked spear-shafts,

dented kettles, frayed hawsers, the moan
of the dying. Hektor and his thugs
could be seen far off, skirmishing, hurling torches,

trying to set the fleet ablaze. A god
might have put on his sunglasses, ignoring
the insect life that goes on below.

Seeing the Trojans come forward like beetles,
I felt a curious fascination, as if I were rubbernecking
at some fender bender. It was not much of a wall,

mostly piles of trash and sandy embankment.
From its rock perch, a knife-tailed hawk
dropped like a stone. The priests called that

the descent of a god, which was fine
if you followed some filthy Eastern religion.
When the Trojans leapt the thrown-together defenses

like ballet dancers, the gods were nowhere.
The Greeks, well, they fought like Greeks,
shields overlapping like fish scales,

helmets touching like men in bed together,
their ridiculous shakos chopped from horse tails;
but against us slouched the leviathan Hektor,

morbidly obese, as hard to stop as a dump truck.
Men battled in pairs, singly, swarming in confusion,
like brokers waving their arms on the floor at Wall Street.

Teukros caught one of Priam's sons-in-law
with a spearpoint below the ear,
just where the carotid fetches into the brain.

The blood hosed every man in range.
Then a long spear came wheezing through the lines.
Teukros ducked and the harpoon caught Amphimachos

below the breastbone. It was that funny.
The big man screamed like a girl
and dropped stone dead, his armor clanging like chimes.

Multiply the scene a hundred times. Hell, a thousand.
Men cut the heads off fresh corpses,
then rolled them through the lines like bowling balls.

Our kings stole armor from the rotting dead
and tossed it in a slave's direction. That was just
another way of doing business. On went the fandango

through the afternoon, the afternoons,
chariots wheeling, horses hamstrung
along the shingle, gutted men beside them

broken up like toys, and the poets back in Greece
already thumbing up the right metaphor—
say, a lion or a mountain boar, not that the poets

had seen many lions, or mountain boars.
Tuned to the lyre, the death of a warrior
became the felling of a thick-shanked oak.

The poets had learned the wisdom
of getting their war dispatches secondhand.
One after another, the son of so-and-so—

some petty king or minor god
who once had it off with a big-tittied girl—
took a spear to the liver, the gut, the throat,

any place that promised a fountain of blood.
A man cut across the belly
watched his own intestines bloom,

blue as sausages; and another saw
his cock nipped off neat as a rosebud.
No one dared say, *This is weird—it's just like a movie.*

It was *better* than special effects.
If you believed the eleven o'clock news, the gods
saw everything, masked as at Mardi Gras—

they veiled their favorites when the dancing got thick,
casting up mysterious steams of camouflage.
I saw a lot of men die, often slowly,

squealing for their mothers. I knew more than a few
of those boys, and one or two with reputations;
but, a year later, who could point out

exactly where some apple-cheeked Myrmidon
stopped breathing, his chest sliced open
as if by a scalpel, so you could see the pink pleats

of his lungs, the purple sturgeon of his liver?
No one could remember his last words,
or if he whispered any through the blood.

I laughed when Menelaos coldcocked Peisandros
with an ax, making his eyes pop out,
then made a speech, the way soldiers do in poems,

the death stretched out on hexameter like a tanned hide,
though in battle mostly you heard
FUCK, FUCK, FUCK, FUCK, FUCK!

There were other things, Ajax the Oak
beaning Hektor with a rock, like Bob Feller,
or standing shoulder to shoulder with Ajax the Shrub

like a yoke of oxen, fighting all comers,
shouting witty repartee like comic-book superheroes.
Or the mornings the arrows came down

like exclamation points. Even so, the Trojans
almost got the best of it. In the end,
a few stuck-up heroes received their comeuppance.

Hera charged a wristful of gold bangles
to Zeus's credit card. But let me tell you
how the wind turned helices through the shifting leaves.

Four Fragments of the *Odyssey*

i. *The Death of Elpenor*

I brought my men away except Elpenor,
our little brother, no good at a sea knot
or a sea fight, and without a lick of sense.
Restless and drunk, he reeled away from the fire,
off to a dusty corner where he could drowse
away from the jabber, out in the sea breeze.
He found some straw on the flat roof of the palace.
At dawn he heard the noise of the other sailors,
joking and swearing, scraping their gear together,
forgot where he was, forgot the rickety ladder,
and half asleep walked blindly into the air.
His neck bone snapped like a dove's, and he was dead.

[X: 551–560]

ii. *The Cattle of Helios*

They swayed. The fork-horned oxen cropped the weeds
beneath the shadow of the black prow.
The dark Greeks waded through the herd, slapping their rumps,
and chased a pair of oxen up the beach.
Surrounding them, the warriors spoke to their gods
and stripped the new leaves from a bristling oak—
there was no barley left within the ship.
They slit the cattle's throats, one at a time,
and flayed their hides. Thick blood soaked the sand.
Cutting away the meat, they wrapped the thighs in fat,
and in the double folds laid gobbets of flesh.

They had no wine to pour on the steaming guts—
tipping a leather bucket of freezing brine,
they scorched the stinking things in the low fire.
When the fatty meat had burnt, and the guts were coals,
they spitted on their spears the bloody steaks.
I had been asleep. I wobbled down the shore,
back to the ship, and smelled an unfamiliar smell.
I knew then what my hungry men had done,
and spoke to Zeus in all my gristly rage
for drugging me with sleep, and letting my companions
draw their bronze knives, and kill the sacred cattle.

[XII: 354–373]

iii. *The Return to Kharybdis*

The air reeked sulfur. Knocked overboard, my men
ghosted down the waves, cawing like sea crows.
A dark god stole their lives and their passage home.
I staggered aft, where waves had torn out the keel.
The rigging was gone, except a rawhide backstay,
and with it I lashed the keel to the shattered mast.
As the ship broke up, I rode them into the waves.
The west wind faltered, then the south picked up,
and back my crude raft drifted toward Kharybdis,
through the cold froth of tar-black night. At dawn,
the sun broke on the jagged rock of Skylla,
and below it the whirlpool sucked down seawater.
I could just reach the bole of a sea fig—
as the mast dropped away, I hung like a bat,
the branches drooping far over the whirlpool,
the knotted mass of roots out of reach. I clung there,
waiting for Kharybdis to spew up the mast.

All day I dangled, arms racked in their sockets,
almost till dark, when a man, still in his robes,
leaves the law court for supper, having judged
the dreary cases brought by violent young men
eager to sue their neighbors, even their friends—
then mast and keel, still tangled, burst to the surface.
I fell on them and weakly paddled away.

[XII: 417–444]

iv. *The Kidnapping of Eumaios*

One of the mates showed up at my father's house
wearing a gold chain hung with amber teardrops.
He laid it in my mother's cool, soft hands.
Turning it in her fingers, she asked the price,
showing her servants how it caught the light—
and as it glowed, he nodded to my nurse.
Late in the day, she led me from the palace,
past the great table where my father's men
had drunk away the hours before the debates.
She slipped three hammered goblets in her robe—
I followed her in my cold innocence.
Late afternoon, the streets were long in shadow.
We took the rutted road to the flashing harbor,
where the Phoenician ship lay rocking at anchor
like a carving knife. Traders took us aboard,
and we cut the salt-whipped sea on a trailing wind.
Days passed. A week. The coast was just in sight.
Clutching her chest, my nurse staggered as if shot,
and pitched facedown in the bilge like a diving tern.
The sailors threw her corpse to the barking seals,
and brought me here to Ithaka, where I was sold.

[XV: 459–483]

AFTER SAPPHO 31

That guy over there, lounging like a god,
gets to listen to you natter on prettily
or giggle in a way that makes
        my blood pressure rise.

Whenever I get a glimpse of you,
I can't think of a thing to say—
my skin smolders with St. Elmo's fire,
        my glasses fog up,

my ears roar, I get the cold sweats,
and my face turns white as winter grass.
Baby, I'm just that much closer then
        to dying.

AFTER SAPPHO 58

Girls, if you want to be immortal, you'd better start
scribbling pop songs, or pick up a guitar.

I used to have a body to die for—now my fingers are knots
of arthritis. I'm still a baby-faced brunette, but my roots are white.

My heart's a mailbox. My knees need replacement surgery,
though back in the day I danced the stage at Woodstock.

Nobody likes to get old, but what can a girl do?
Soon you have wrinkles no plastic surgeon can hide.

Once a movie star flew her toy boy to the South Pole
and put him in cold storage. She was caught red-handed.

He was handsome as Brad Pitt then. Look at him now,
gray-haired and using Viagra, while she doesn't have crow's-feet.

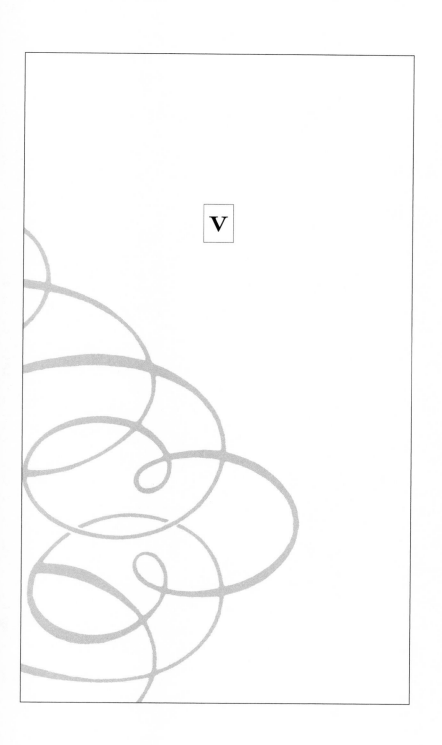

V

RSVP

Come as you are

The Stoics knew the solitudes of will
are what we pay for this box-office lease.
Please let me come as what I wish I were,
as Cary Grant, Brad Pitt, or Cyd Charisse.

ALONG THE AUTUMN RIVER

Westport Point, Massachusetts

Willows. I was thinking of the willows,
their clean, unregarding green, the ruffled purity

that decorated the muddy banks of our sluggish,
forever autumnal river, its wharf long weathered

to a philosophical gloom, rotted docks
contemplating a few orphaned pilings,

the stumps of a drowned forest.
On the shore, unpainted dories lay overturned,

like gray Jurassic beetles, the barnacled hulls
stoved in perhaps by a disconsolate owner.

They had carried squat barrels of molasses
or casks of oil, the humble cartage of the northern docks.

Even in those latter days, draggers hauled anchor
for the Georges Bank, then still running with cod.

The broad-hipped river was our Mississippi.
None of us realized that the cornucopia

awash in the wharf's galvanized bins—the clams
like dull lumps of silver; the brute, delicate lobsters—

would one day vanish like the horse and buggy,
the manual typewriter, the long-playing record.

THE CRANE AMONG ITS MINIONS

Like a chalk-white spire
rising over the Herefords of the Beef Teaching Unit,
the whooping crane stood alone with the alone,

its rackety rattle half whistle, half war whoop.
Sandhill cranes milled around it like Myrmidons.
Only one man can be an Agamemnon—

everyone else is an also-ran, and still may not survive.
The barbed wire glinted like spearpoints.
The sun blazed like a hammered shield.

Puffy clouds seeped above us like blisters,
the Florida days ten years too long,
Januaries with too much *Sturm und Drang*, or too little.

And there he stood, the great bird with his war crest—
regal, scientific, nervous without nerve—
while the many stood watching an old-fashioned god.

On the Wood Storks

Behind the movie theater's neon *beau monde*
cooled the dank waters of a retention pond,

cyclone-fenced, palm-guarded, overgrown.
You walked there when you wanted to be alone.

For weeks nothing stirred the blackened reeds,
which were enough, those days you felt the need.

Then, one evening, through the gathered gloom,
as if something uncanny had entered a room,

across algae green as an Alpine meadow,
eight white ghosts floated faintly through the shadow,

pausing, worrying, then slowly moving on,
the waters like a chessboard scattered with white pawns.

When bankers review their fat portfolios,
they draw their dark beaks open and closed,

great shears to cut some invisible thread.
The pale birds stalked like something newly dead.

One lifted a black-edged wing, in search of food,
and somehow that broke your somber mood.

Yet on they marched, like Dante's souls through Hell,
awaiting the Last Judgment's redeeming bell,

working their way in silence, fallen aristocrats.
You said they looked like ladies' hats,

white as the color of love, if love has color—
bright white, you meant, only a little duller.

BLUES

I got a fish, you know he want to hide.
I got a spotty fish, you know he want to hide.
He swim upstream in the water, Lord,
        never swim side to side.

I got a hound, that dog love to hunt.
I got a coonhound, that dog love to hunt.
He know that black swamp so bad, Lord,
        he love her back to front.

I got a gun, can't get him to shoot.
I got a rusty gun, can't never get him to shoot.
When Eve shoot that gun in the Bible, Lord,
        they call him forbidden fruit.

I got a Cadillac car, she won't drive for me.
I got a shiny black Cadillac, she won't drive for me.
You take her out on the highway, Lord,
        she sing like she got the Ph.D.

I got a woman, she give me no love.
I got a big woman, never give me no love.
But when that sweet woman whisper, Lord,
        I tremble like the sky above.

Dies Irae

> For days and days we voyaged along, through seas so wearily, lone-
> somely mild, that all space, in repugnance to our vengeful errand,
> seemed vacating itself of life before our urn-like prow.
>
> —*Moby-Dick*

Glory days! And not so glorious.
The usual more unusual, the older you get,

a diplomatic woodpecker lingering in the eye
after the tree is bare. At dawn, the residual dawn,

a leafy sun casts a lozenge of shadow.
Dead these three years, the neighbor,

or the hovering bird of his ghost,
mewls like the damned, whose gnashing

laments upon the Sistine wall
were said to disturb the whisper of matins.

When gray-haired strangers buried my mother's urn,
they claimed even the ashes were polite.

On the Suburbs

So soon as we profess to be Christ's soldiers, as a malicious and fierce enemy [the devil] invadeth us.

—Edwin Sandys, 1574

i. Comic Relief Could Still Be Found in Bed

What were our chances with the CIA?
We tore the posters down before we left—
to publish in the run-up to the war
gave us a box seat on the glorious past.
The Party laptops threatened the altarpiece,
beheaded statues, burnt the sacred boots.
Designer perfumes declared their loyalty
but in the darkness managed to drift away.
Seductive whispers had brought fate to heel.
At last, submission proved the only choice—
women were handcuffed in French lingerie,
the hands of midnight raised in bold surrender.
The windows listened, but the door replied.

ii. *The Words We Needed Couldn't Find Their Way*

Through the bay windows lay an unnamed road,
a fortune-teller, boy bands, ATMs.
No one imagined that the seas would rise
or moles lay down their burdens on the lawn.
Pit bulls spoke fluently in Mandarin,
but working cell phones were considered rare.
While in new parks flares guttered and expired
under dry stars that juddered in despair,
informers scoured the woods for the *haute bourgeoisie*.
What if the censors banned the apricot?
Out-of-work actors took their billfolds out
and paused in silence to forget their parts.
Rivers refused to learn the postal codes.

iii. *The Ink Still Lingered on the Lover's Cheek*

Mr. and Mrs. did not stay the course.
They spouted nonsense in the church and mall,
perjured their laundry, torched the Cadillac,
cheated on taxes, bought two graveyard plots.
They owned the farm, the bluetick hounds in bed,
the fresh-laid Parian flagstones by the pool—
nothing was moral but the watered lawn.
On Amateur Night, rumors of birth consumed
the quiet lane. Bodyguards were recalled,
some passports seized, but tickets left uncanceled.
What manger could their secrets now inhabit?
The defects of their natures were invincible,
standing on the piazza of a dream.

iv. New Resolutions Lost the Central Zones

Radical youth still kept its badges shined,
sweeping down catwalks with a damp hauteur,
their top hats cocked, Hermès scarves knotted tight.
If in the cellar lay the fountain of youth,
the obscure restaurant thought it wrong to tell.
(Nothing they promised made us drink Bordeaux.)
New model visions danced before the hourglass.
Children raised Halloween masks to their faces
and spoke in tongues. The sundial stopped at six.
Though wanted-posters shivered on sheetrock walls,
cold rains gave up the past and paid a price.
One by one, the servants crawled home to ask
why the new monsters did not know their names.

ON THE HEDGEHOG

The screech, screech, screech,
like the plainchant of a cell phone,
was merely the local hedgehog
licking clean his cracked saucer.

Nights he tottered unsteadily
through ghost bracken and thorn,
the board fence overgrown and scientific—
a skeletal bike rusted to its stand,

the moon spending its last quarter.
About his Oliver Twist diet,
he refused to complain, shyly
scraping the china across the paving stones.

The sky lightens to a deep monotone,
and it's time to be fleeing, O alley Cybele!
You know the wages of quiet,
Night Prince of brick and mortar.

The unexamined life, what is it meant to be like?
Just one long beatific
gaze beneath a crown of thorns,
then through the shadows like a scribble by Doré?

No one asked you to like Chaucer,
or Grendel who rose from a bog,
a monster who by gesture or bearing alone . . .
but you too love the failures of speech.

Atlantic Ocean. Winter. 1954.

The surface trembled,
bluish like a hammered sheet of tin.
Clouds in the broad sky lay like rips in old linen.
Already insurance adjusters were pulling up in black cars.

Winter in the Old School

Even the ravens suffered from insolence,
those December afternoons. Cold and soon colder,

the tall sky prepared its come-hither look.
You napped through the brief days from dawn to dusk,

shadows unrolling into the icy streets
like some orchestral prelude. Night

turned clerical or industrious. Yet there we were,
sipping cup after cup of hot water,

with no religious taste, or very little,
and thinking, like the English, in complete sentences.

The Old Story

After the Blitz, her mother had begun an affair. So she said.
No one would have called her well-bred,

but she knew how to fill a low-cut dress,
had a fetching smile and a tongue for success.

He was a promising actor named Domenic,
or Paul—a Polish exile, perhaps. A few thick

letters survive, now water-stained and torn,
from the month after the baby was born.

They are his daughter's unhappy souvenirs.
Her mother lied through the difficult years,

when she would speak of him at all.
As a girl, R. thought her father the dashing tall

naval commander whose picture her mother flashed
at Christmas. Oh, that bushy mustache!

(Merely a distant cousin, and not the smartest.)
Later, the old girl modeled for a few flamboyant artists,

coarser and more imperious as her figure spread,
a Borgia to her family before she was dead,

never betraying a secret or forgetting a slight.
Her whole life could be traced to one brief night.

And the young actor, who trod the boards
at Sadler's Wells, swinging a fake sword?

History, that Chanel-clad thief, averts her eyes,
in cruelty, perhaps, with the usual sighs.

Winter of Falling Temperature

Frost settled on the vines like powdered sugar.
The city took its time. What was dawn

but a crosshatch of old scenes until scarred new?
Crystals furred the glass like lichen,

leached into the new forest's albino flowers.
Mirrors of ice lay shattered along gutters.

Spring fell narrowly ahead,
some worn-out land with outspread harbors

and waving beauties. What was the punishment
Dante reserved for traitors? Only the Frigidaire.

Bitterness seeped through our bedroom walls,
not silvery like passion,

but like a child who never intended to be born.

The Imitation of Things Familiar

England

At dawn, the doves practice their imitation of owls
or their American cousins, featureless as souls.

How did they spot us, fresh off airport ramps,
our passports steaming with new stamps?

The girls from the sixth-form college look
bedraggled and oppressed, as if they took

from school no more than names and dates.
Everything, for them, has happened too late—

the dead are just their secret sharers.
Like all things built of love, the past is whispers.

Or is it like water, indifferent and cruel,
poured into a language strange as Istanbul?

As we get older, we stare into all-too-deep abysses.
The pool we love was once loved by Narcissus.

WINTER WITHOUT MEMORY

From the bricked arch of the Victorian bridge,
we gazed down the muddy lane,

channeled through the yews with a carpenter's eye,
as dusk slowly took the skies behind us.

Once the path had been a spur line
to some pensioned-off village in the fens

now bloated with London commuters.
The almost-dusk whisper of dusk—

was the hue the dead leaf of oak or poplar?
In that suspension of genial air,

tasting like smoke as smoke tastes like regret,
down the lane, tail up like a maid's

understairs brush, trotted a fox
with the bolt of purpose in its mouth.

To the Ghost of an Old Girlfriend

> Let it be as though a man could go backwards through death.
> —Donald Justice

Tell me of that night in the weeds,
the lace panties around your thin ankles,
of the scent of shame, like some heady insecticide.
Tell me of the weather there, if the storms
come brute and calamitous, or if they linger,
casting down day after day of rain, not tinged with acid
but relentless, smelling slightly of mildew.
Tell me why I have forgotten your face.

The afternoon will be brief, punctuated
by mosquitoes, the swamps moody in the distance.
Appear as the young woman you were, blonde
and nineteen, or as some rueful, gray-haired stranger,
full of accusation and desire.

What is Florida, after all,
but where Charon patrols the fishing camps
to embark the dead, poling his flatboat
into mangrove swamps under the crêpe of Spanish moss?

Men squat around low fires, drinking the cheapest beer.
Fishing lines have been strung
into the moldy water, while offshore a couple of alligators
slump, awaiting developments. Angels
have teeth no more razorlike and appetites
no keener. They too stare with the predator's
patience, their eyes glowing red after sunset.

Show me your passport, so I can trace the obscure stamps
or imagine you in some doomed suburb of Schenectady,
near the broken gas pumps of a 7-Eleven,
still nursing your wounds—or was that your pride?
Tell me if that was your life, or only the prelude to life.
Tell me why we were innocents before and not after.

THE OTHER PLACE

The leaves had fallen in that sullen place,
but none around him knew just where they were.
The sky revealed no sun. A ragged blur
remained where each man's face had been a face.

Two angels soon crept forth with trays of bread,
circling among the lost like prison guards.
Love is not love, unless it still affords
forgiveness for the words that are not said.

He simply could not believe that this was Hell,
that others sent before him did not know;
yet, once his name and memory grew faint,
it was no worse, perhaps, than a cheap motel.
It is the love of failure makes a saint.
He stood up then, but did not try to go.

A Death at Badenweiler

1904

Moscow! You should have seen the city then!
Even in winter, the slate-blue river locked
in ice below the Kremlin walls, the glaring
plain of small boats frozen against the banks,
the crowds in lush fur-capes or threadbare shawls
flowed through the shadowed streets as one black current,
the city blazing like a photograph.

Cities like Moscow can be too much with you;
they are too great, as other cities are
too small. We found ourselves in Badenweiler
that July, my brother nerve-dead with exhaustion—
nothing, the doctors claimed, but his exams.
We had fled south, south, to the smoky hills
of the Black Forest, smudged like a fairy tale.
The season then was running near the flood,
the preening crowds in frills of summer dress
making slow progress down the promenades
that pierced the town, to see and to be seen,
like those who in *Persuasion* swanned the walks.
The curtained dining room of our hotel
let us stand witness to the sweeping entrée
of a great actress we had known in Moscow.
Turned from the door of one august establishment,
Frau C. and her husband had been forced to take
an airless chamber that overlooked the street;
yet, to their sharp relief, that stifling day,
with the most gracious show of courtesy,
the hotel manager sent in his card

to ask if they would view a quiet room
that chance had just then made available.
Her fox-faced husband had been ill all spring;
when the old wracking demons came upon him,
from his pocket he removed—*très élégant*,
sealed tight, wholly discreet—a blue spittoon
(for that sole reason had their first hotel
abruptly withdrawn its hospitality).
Though tanned, even robust, the invalid
already bore a haunted, feral look.
He fancied a lazy tour of the Crimea
and had me order him two flannel suits,
cream with a blue stripe, then a blue with cream.
Those afternoons, I read him Russian papers,
the pages black with bulletins from Japan.

One humid midnight, I woke to frantic knocks.
Shivering upon my threshold stood Frau C.,
clad in a dressing gown, wringing her hands,
face pale as a ghost's. My hair in disarray,
I blundered through uncertain balmy streets,
stumbling at last on her doctor's unlit gate.
I rang the small brass bell. A sleepy growl
rose from the silence, to silence then descended,
cursing my name. I was dispatched at once
to fetch a cylinder of oxygen
from a chemist comically still in his nightcap.
The sickroom's gas lamps had been turned down low.
Herr C. lay propped on mounts of feather pillows,
gasping for air, hoarse as the newly damned—
his cough had nearly carried him away.
Terrible wheezes clawed his weakened body
until all breath had vanished from the room.

The young physician, whose gallant manner mocked
the dueling scar cut deep into one cheek,
bent down to listen to the poor man's lungs.
He snapped his fingers at the sleepy porter,
demanding a chilled bottle of champagne.
Filling the crystal flutes near to the brim,
the doctor gaily offered one to C.
Though weak, he plucked the crystal up and rasped,
"How long since I last had a taste of this?"
then drained the contents in a fearsome gulp.
No sooner was it done, the glass just placed
on the near table, forming a tableau
like a cheap oil by Cézanne, when a slight hiss,
a comic gassy gurgle—such as a tap
makes when the air is trapped—burst from his mouth.
Sleepy at last, he turned upon his side,
supported by his wife, her swanlike neck
glowing in gaslight as the room grew still.
The sick man dozed. The crisis past, I thought
we all could sleep. The doctor held his hand,
long fingers playing lightly on Herr C.'s
skeletal wrist, as if to check the pulse.
Soon, shrugging his shoulders, the good doctor stood,
saying, "It's over now. Our friend is gone."
Frau C. wept in great shudders in my arms.
Her husband's remains were carted off at once,
borne half-reclining in a linen basket
in order not to disturb the other guests.
Everyone knew his plays, of course, the stories,
though I myself have never troubled to read them.

Years later, I was told, in such a case,
when hope is lost, physicians have a sign,
a mortal code they use between themselves.
Champagne is always what the doctor orders.

After Sappho

We would call her Psappha, were it a matter of dialect; but that is mere sentimentality, a wish to make the past strange again. In our cunning and duplicitous relations with the past, we are shadows chasing shadows; worse, we are shadows burdened by our luggage. With Sappho, we know her only by report of report, like gunshot echoing another gunshot, until a message is borne across a country.

The poet comes to us out of that obscure Greek period between Homer and Plato—of Homer we know nothing of use; with Plato, a man begins to emerge from the dust of the historical. Sappho's poems were highly regarded during her life (some critics would make her the Sharon Olds of her day) and for long afterward. It's said that they fell out of fashion only when her Aeolic dialect became too difficult for the Byzantine school curriculum. The very few complete poems we have survived by accident; even now, from the sands of Oxyrhynchus and elsewhere, shreds of papyrus, the waste matter wrapping the bodies of the dead, make their way to the surface. If we bound our own dead in the pages of books, the future would have a peculiar sense of our literary tastes—what modern age wants to be known by its best sellers?

In 2004, two scholars reported the discovery of a scrap of papyrus that allowed an almost complete restoration of what had been known to Sappho scholars as "Fragment 58." The following year, an article in the *Times Literary Supplement* by Martin West gave a provisional restoration of the whole poem, for which he offered his own translation. This was followed some weeks later by translations by Lachlan Mackinnon and Edwin Morgan, also in *TLS,* and that fall by Anne Carson in the *New York Review of Books.* My own translation took another tack—I wanted to give Sappho a modern idiom, yet follow as closely as possible the thinking of the original. This is a mug's game; but I have learned more about Homer from Christopher Logue's madness than from the sanities of half a dozen other translations of the *Iliad.* I have paid homage to his work in "Book Thirteen." Some shards of translation that stay closer to the original, though not without a strain of wildness, follow in "Four Fragments of the *Odyssey.*"

I have titled the translation "After Sappho 58," with due regard for its status as imitation and its belated presence, long after her words were lost to the sands. I undertook this translation with caution, not least because ancient Greek is the poorest of my ragged languages. Later I added a similar translation of "Sappho 31." Perhaps there is something to be gained from approaching the past with a sense of inadequacy, and a chip on your shoulder.

About the Author

WILLIAM LOGAN has published ten volumes of poetry and five volumes of essays and reviews. *The Undiscovered Country* won the National Book Critics Circle Award in Criticism. He lives in Gainesville, Florida, and Cambridge, England.

Penguin Poets